NUGGETS FROM
Song of Songs

BONIFACE DAAWIEH-KEELSON

NUGGETS FROM
Song of Songs

Family Life Series

NUGGETS FROM
SONG OF SONGS

BONIFACE DAAWIEH-KEELSON

Published for Worldwide Distribution by:
QUEST PUBLICATIONS
6-176 Henry Street
Brantford, Ontario, N3S 5C8
Canada
Email: questpublications@outlook.com
Website: www.questpub.questforgod.org

Cover Design & Interior Layout / Formatting by:
QUEST PUBLICATIONS

ISBN-13: 978-1-988439-07-5

To share your testimonies with me please write to me on
this address:
Boniface Daawieh-Keelson
DarwiehBooks and Publications
P.O. Box AF 657, Adenta-Accra,
Ghana, West Africa

OR Contact me on the following Cell Phones
001-233 244765586
001-233 244684802

My other contacts are Email:
amawaa@yahoo.com
evangelistboniface@ymail.com
bonifacekeelson@gmail.com

Social Media:
www.facebook.com/boniface.keelson
www.facebook.com/boniface.keelson

All scripture quotations are from the King James Version
of the Bible unless otherwise stated.

Contents

INTRODUCTION

Song of Solomon is one book in the Bible that is scarcely read by Christians and hardly preached from by preachers. It has a lot of unfamiliar expressions and appears a bit confusing to many. There are a number of characters in the book but principally, it is about a certain Shunamite woman and her husband (or husband-to-be). Whilst some commentators believe this husband was Solomon, others believe the husband was an unknown and unnamed shepherd boy in the fields. However, there is no debate to the fact that King Solomon wrote this book.

King Solomon was such great man. God blessed him so much with wisdom and insight. He wrote very powerful and inspiring proverbs, poems and songs.

The Bible says he wrote 1,005. One of the 1,005 songs he wrote is the book "Song of Solomon". As mentioned earlier, the Book is primarily a chronicle of the conversation of a husband and his wife. Using the book for our family devotion recently, my wife and I came across several life application nuggets especially from the conversation of the couple which are very applicable for family life (for husbands and wives). These are the nuggets I share with you in this book.

GOD BLESS YOU!
BONIFACE

CHAPTER 1

THE ATMOSPHERE OF LOVE

1. MOUTH TO MOUTH KISSES ARE MEANT ABSOLUTELY FOR COUPLES.

Let him kiss me with the kisses of his mouth: for thy love is better than wine. (Song of Solomon 1:2 KJV)

Never engage with mouth to mouth kissing with someone who is not your spouse. It is an act meant only for a husband and wife. Many people have been initiated through mouth to mouth kissing with dangerous personalities parading as normal persons.

2. A WIFE MUST INVITE THE KISSES OF HER HUSBAND.

Let him kiss me with the kisses of his mouth: for thy love is better than wine. (Song of Solomon 1:2 KJV)

Smile, welcome the kisses and pecks of your husband, and stop pushing him away.

3. HUSBANDS AND WIVES MUST MAKE THEMSELVES KISSABLE.

Let him kiss me with the kisses of his mouth: for thy love is better than wine. (Song of Solomon 1:2 KJV)

Look good, keep your dental cavity clean and fresh, smile often, have good breath and be ever ready to give or receive a kiss or a peck from your spouse.

4. THE ATMOSPHERE OF LOVE IS WHAT EVERY WIFE SINCERELY DESIRES.

...thy love is better than wine...we will be glad and rejoice in thee, we will remember thy love more than wine: the upright love thee. (Song of Solomon 1:2b, 4c KJV)

Like wine, the atmosphere of love is exhilarating and stimulating. Ensure that there is love in your home. Treat your wife and family with love and respect. Cherish them dearly. This is an atmosphere for a healthy home.

5. AN ATMOSPHERE OF LOVE TRULY SATISFIES AND SPICES UP MARITAL RELATIONSHIP.

...thy love is better than wine...we will be glad and rejoice in thee, we will remember thy love more than wine: the upright love thee. (Song of Solomon 1:2b, 4c KJV)

The atmosphere of love in a home truly satisfies. A wife and a family that experiences love at home are always fulfilled and satisfied. With such love they may not need wine or pleasures from other people or sources. Never destroy the atmosphere of love in your home.

6. GOOD BODY ODOUR IS A VERY IMPORTANT INGREDIENT THAT SPICE UP RELATIONSHIP OF COUPLES.

Because of the savour of thy good ointments thy name is as ointment poured forth, therefore do the virgins love thee. (Song of Solomon 1:3 KJV)

A pleasant body smell is very significant in a marital union. Never joke with your bath. Bath well and properly. Fight body odour. Shower before you go to bed. It is essential in marriage.

7. A HUSBAND WITH GOOD AND GODLY VIRTUES IS WHAT EVERY WIFE (EVERY WOMAN) PRAYS FOR.

Because of the savour of thy good ointments thy name is as ointment poured forth, therefore do the virgins love thee. (Song of Solomon 1:3 KJV)

The wife (in this text) compares her husband's good and godly virtues to fragrant ointment, and concludes that it is the main reason why all the virgins love him and wish he is their beloved. Do not throw away your good and godly values as a husband. And if you have none, please cultivate some.

8. EVERY GOOD HUSBAND KNOWS THE WORTH OF HIS NAME (PARTICULARLY TO HIS WIFE).

Because of the savour of thy good ointments thy name is as ointment poured

forth, therefore do the virgins love thee.
(Song of Solomon 1:3 KJV)

In marriage most wives drop their surnames for the husband's surname. That alone must tell any husband the significance of maintaining a good name in this life. In our study, the name of the husband was very dear to his wife—."thy name is as ointment poured forth". Your name stands for who you are and all that you stand for. Protect your name well!

9. EVERY WIFE YEARNS FOR CLOSE FELLOWSHIP WITH THE HUSBAND.

Draw me, we will run after thee: the king hath brought me into his chambers: we will be glad and rejoice in thee, we will remember thy love more than wine: the upright love thee. (Song of Solomon 1:4 KJV)

The expression 'draw me' in the text points out that need and desire. The secret and inner cry of most wives is for their husbands to draw them into closer fellowship at all times.

10. A TRUE HUSBAND MUST HAVE WHAT IT TAKES TO DRAW THE WIFE ALONG IN LIFE.

Draw me, we will run after thee: the king hath brought me into his chambers: we will be glad and rejoice in thee, we will remember thy love more than wine: the upright love thee. (Song of Solomon 1:4 KJV)

A husband is suppose to lead. A wife is suppose to follow. As a leader the husband must have what it takes to draw the wife along. It must function like a magnet not by force. For example, a husband must set goals and standards for the family and draw his wife and his family along.

11. A REAL WIFE MUST SINCERELY LEARN TO RUN (FOLLOW) AFTER THE HUSBAND.

Draw me, we will run after thee: the king hath brought me into his chambers: we will be glad and rejoice in thee, we will remember thy love more than wine: the upright love thee. (Song of Solomon 1:4 KJV)

A good wife must humble herself and submissively go along with the husband. She must allow the husband to lead. It is difficult for two captains to pilot a ship. Bring out your ideas and suggestions in a submissive manner as a wife. And even where you are the originator of an idea, hide yourself behind and push your husband ahead and follow from behind.

12. GREAT HUSBANDS LEAD HUMBLE AND SUBMISSIVE WIVES FOLLOW.

Draw me, we will run after thee: the king hath brought me into his chambers: we will be glad and rejoice in thee, we will remember thy love more than wine: the upright love thee. (Song of Solomon 1:4 KJV)

It is very frustrating for a wife to follow a husband who have no vision and who do not know how to lead his family. It is equally frustrating for a husband to lead a wife who is an activist of equal rights and not humble enough to follow the leadership of a husband.

13. A HUSBAND MUST BE A ROLE MODEL TO HIS HOUSEHOLD.

Draw me, we will run after thee: the king hath brought me into his chambers: we will be glad and rejoice in thee, we will remember thy love more than wine: the upright love thee. (Song of Solomon 1:4 KJV)

As a husband you may not be able to become a role model to the world, to your country, or to your community. Nevertheless, you must become a role model to your wife and to your household.

14. A WIFE MUST WORK ON LOOKING GOOD NO MATTER THE STATE SHE IS IN.

I am black, but comely, O ye daughters of Jerusalem, as the tents of Kedar, as the curtains of Solomon. (Song of Solomon 1:5 KJV)

You can be black and yet comely. No matter your state as a wife you must do your best to look good. The fact that you are a mother of three must not make you live like a grandmother. Your new shape must not deter you from looking good. Even your advanced age must not keep you from looking good. Remember the key word is 'look good' and not look like a camouflage. Please do not bleach, and do not dress like a shameless woman.

15. LEARN NOT TO BLAME YOURSELF FOR WHAT IS NOT YOUR DOING.

Look not upon me, because I am black, because the sun hath looked upon me: my mother's children were angry with me; they made me the keeper of the vineyards; but mine own vineyard have I not kept. (Song of Solomon 1:6 KJV)

Please stop blaming yourself for a number of things you have no control over. According to the wife in the text, her being dark was as a result of the effect of the sun and hard labour. If your shape is affected as a result of child birth please don't 'kill yourself'. If a cause in life which you have no control over obstructs your dream please do not blame yourself.

16. NEVER BLAME YOUR SPOUSE FOR WHAT IS NOT HIS OR HER DOING.

Look not upon me, because I am black, because the sun hath looked upon me: my mother's children were angry with me; they made me the keeper of the vineyards; but mine own vineyard have I not kept. (Song of Solomon 1:6 KJV)

Stop blaming your spouse for what is not his or her doing. For instance, do not blame your spouse when he is doing his best but is unable to make it like others. Do not blame your wife if she has no big buttocks like other women.

17. THE ISSUE OF OTHER CHILDREN IN A MARITAL RELATIONSHIP IS ALWAYS

AN ISSUE, PLEASE LOOK BEFORE YOU LEAP.

Look not upon me, because I am black, because the sun hath looked upon me: my mother's children were angry with me; they made me the keeper of the vineyards; but mine own vineyard have I not kept. (Song of Solomon 1:6 KJV)

According to the 'wife' in this text, her half siblings hated her and treated her bad. Before entering into any marriage know for sure that where there are other children it could certainly become a matter of concern. Do not over look it. In a marriage where there are other children parents must be careful how they incorporate all of them.

18. YOUR OWN VINEYARD (MARRIAGE) MUST BE YOUR MOST IMPORTANT PRIORITY.

Look not upon me, because I am black, because the sun hath looked upon me: my mother's children were angry with me; they made me the keeper of the vineyards; but mine own vineyard have I not kept. (Song of Solomon 1:6 KJV)

In life priorities are very significant. Be more concern about yourself before caring for others. Think of your marriage first. Treat your children good before your nieces and nephews. One advice in an aircraft always is that, 'in case of emergency fix your own oxygen max before fixing that of your child or someone else'. The wife in the text complains that circumstances beyond her control caused her to be busy taking care of other peoples vineyard, that she had no time to take care of her own (especially her physical appearance)

19. A WIFE HAS THE RIGHT TO KNOW ALL ABOUT HER HUSBAND'S BUSINESS, ESTATES, PURSUIT, INVESTMENTS, MOVEMENTS ETC.

Tell me, O thou whom my soul loveth, where thou feedest, where thou makest thy flock to rest at noon: for why should I be as one that turneth aside by the flocks of thy companions? (Song of Solomon 1:7 KJV)

In the text, the wife asked to find out where the husband was working. A wife must necessarily know the estate of her husband, where he works, and all his movements.

20. A HUSBAND MUST DISCLOSE EVERYTHING ABOUT HIS BUSINESS,

MOVEMENTS, ESTATES, PURSUIT TO THE WIFE.

Tell me, O thou whom my soul loveth, where thou feedest, where thou makest thy flock to rest at noon: for why should I be as one that turneth aside by the flocks of thy companions? If thou know not, O thou fairest among women, go thy way forth by the footsteps of the flock, and feed thy kids beside the shepherds' tents. (Song of Solomon 1:7-8 KJV)

Please Mr. Husband do not hide things from your wife. Disclose everything about yourself, your family, your business, your estates and investments, and your movements to your wife.

21. A HUSBAND MUST MAKE HIS WIFE A SHAREHOLDER OR A PARTAKER OF

EVERY VENTURE OR ENTERPRISE HE IS INTO.

Tell me, O thou whom my soul loveth, where thou feedest, where thou makest thy flock to rest at noon: for why should I be as one that turneth aside by the flocks of thy companions? If thou know not, O thou fairest among women, go thy way forth by the footsteps of the flock, and feed thy kids beside the shepherds' tents. (Song of Solomon 1:7-8 KJV)

The husband in this text immediately informed the wife that she has the full rights to partake and share in his enterprise. It is wisdom to make your wife a partner in your enterprise. Not necessarily being in the work or the venture, yet a shareholder and an equal partner in all your business and ventures.

22. A WIFE MUST BE SENSITIVE TO OUTFITS AND DRESS CODE THAT BEFITS HER.

Thy cheeks are comely with rows of jewels, thy neck with chains of gold. We will make thee borders of gold with studs of silver. (Song of Solomon 1:10-11 KJV)

Not every outfit may fit you. The reality is that whatever you wear, someone would remark that you look good, and it fits you. Please go for outfits that truly fits you.

23. A WIFE MUST PAY ATTENTION TO DRESS CODE AND OUTFITS THAT THE HUSBAND RECOMMENDS.

Thy cheeks are comely with rows of jewels, thy neck with chains of gold. We will make thee borders of gold with studs of silver. (Song of Solomon 1:10-11 KJV)

Pay more heed to what your husband says about your dress code. Whatever, outfit your husband does not approve of please reconsider your stand. After all, your number one concern must be to dress for your husband.

N/B: Husbands, please do not force old Ghana Empire dress code on your wives. We live in a 21st century.

24.A HUSBAND MUST TAKE INTEREST AND OCCASIONALLY BUY FOR THE WIFE OUTFITS AND ORNAMENTS HE CONSIDERS BEFITTING TO THE WIFE.

We will make thee borders of gold with studs of silver.
(Song of Solomon 1:11 KJV)

Husbands do not just admire and prescribe outfits for your wives. Do your best to occasionally bless your wives with dresses and ornaments that you know fits good on them.

25. A WIFE MUST BE VERY CONCERNED ABOUT THE CONDITION UNDER WHICH THE MEALS OF THE HUSBAND IS SERVED.

While the king sitteth at his table, my spikenard sendeth forth the smell thereof. (Song of Solomon 1:12 KJV)

Never serve your husband under unhygienic condition. Never serve him with undignified bowls and plates. Serve him like a king. Serve him under a hygienic condition. Serve him in a pleasant atmosphere.

26. GOOD BODY SMELL ENHANCES SEX LIFE IN MARRIAGE.

A bundle of myrrh is my wellbeloved unto me; he shall lie all night betwixt my breasts. (Song of Solomon 1:13 KJV)

A wife would scarcely push off a well refreshed, and a pleasant smelling husband. A well refreshed and good smelling wife is attractive in bed. Do not joke with a pleasant and good smell.

27. GIVE GOOD COMPLEMENTS TO YOUR SPOUSE OFTEN.

A bundle of myrrh is my wellbeloved unto me; he shall lie all night betwixt my breasts. My beloved is unto me as a cluster of camphire in the vineyards of Engedi. Behold, thou art fair, my love; behold, thou art fair; thou hast doves' eyes. Behold, thou art fair, my beloved, yea, pleasant: also our bed is green. (Song of Solomon 1:13-16 KJV)

A good complement to a spouse is like fertilizer to a plant. Do not feel lazy about giving good complements to your spouse, especially your wife. Find something to say to your spouse once a while.

28.A WIFE MUST HAVE "DOVE EYES".

Behold, thou art fair, my love; behold, thou art fair; thou hast doves' eyes. (Song of Solomon 1:15 KJV)

Dove eyes are pure eyes. Dove eyes are eyes that see not bad things. Please Mrs. Wife stop reading unnecessary meanings and seeing so much evil in everything your husband does.

29.A WIFE MUST BE PLEASANT.

Behold, thou art fair, my beloved, yea, pleasant: also our bed is green. (Song of Solomon 1:16 KJV)

No husband wants to be around an unpleasant wife. Be a pleasant wife. Wear gorgeous smiles. Be a happy person to be with. Do not be a nagging wife.

30. A WIFE MUST NEVER PLAY WITH THE UPKEEP OF HER HOUSE ESPECIALLY THE BED SHE AND THE HUSBAND SLEEPS ON.

Behold, thou art fair, my beloved, yea, pleasant: also our bed is green. (Song of Solomon 1:16 KJV)

Your home is your castle. Keep it neat. Keep it pleasant. Keep your rooms tidy—especially your bed room.

CHAPTER 2

WISDOM FOR ALL COUPLES

1. **ONCE YOU CHOOSE A WIFE SHE MUST BECOME TO YOU THE ONLY FLOWER.**

   As the lily among thorns, so is my love among the daughters.
   (Song of Solomon 2:2 KJV)

   Mr Husband, your wife is designed by God to be the only lilly for you. All other women are supposed to be thorns to you.

2. **A WIFE MUST BE AS PLEASANT AS A FLOWER AND MUST NEVER BECOME**

A THORN IN THE FLESH OF THE HUSBAND.

As the lily among thorns, so is my love among the daughters.
(Song of Solomon 2:2 KJV)

As a lilly is a pleasant flower so must a wife be to her husband. Wives be tender, lovely, and pleasant unto your husbands always.

3. ALL HUSBANDS MUST KNOW THAT ANY FORM OF ROMANTIC RELATIONSHIP WITH OTHER WOMEN (THORNS) WOULD SURELY END UP IN HURTS.

As the lily among thorns, so is my love among the daughters.
(Song of Solomon 2:2 KJV)

Because your wife is suppose to be the only lilly and all other women thorns, husbands must avoid any emotional and romantic affections towards other women. If you do Mr husband, you would surly hurt yourself at last.

4. A HUSBAND MUST BE TO THE WIFE AS A SWEET APPLE TREE.

As the apple tree among the trees of the wood, so is my beloved among the sons. I sat down under his shadow with great delight, and his fruit was sweet to my taste. (Song of Solomon 2:3 KJV)

Apples are special fruits cherished by all in this world. A husband is to be pleasant, sweet and special to the wife like an apple fruit.

5. ONCE YOU CHOOSE TO SETTLE WITH A MAN, HE ALONE MUST BECOME TO

**YOU AN APPLE TREE. ALL OTHER MEN
ARE ORDINARY TREES.**

*As the apple tree among the trees of the
wood, so is my beloved among the sons.
I sat down under his shadow with great
delight, and his fruit was sweet to my taste.
(Song of Solomon 2:3 KJV)*

Wives, once you have settled on a
husband count all other men as mere
and unprofitable trees to your course in
life. They may be apple trees to others—
but to you they are Bitter trees, 'Nim
trees' or Wawa boards

**6. A TRUE HUSBAND IS A GREAT
COVERING AND SUPPORT TO THE
WIFE.**

*I sat down under his shadow with great
delight, and his fruit was sweet to my taste.
(Song of Solomon 2:3b KJV)*

A husband is a covering to his wife. True husbands function like that. Their presence in the family and in the lives of their wives is like the shade of a tree in a hot sunny environment. Be a real husband!

7. ONE OF THE GREATEST PLEASURE OF A WIFE IN A HEALTHY MARRIAGE IS THE COMPANY OF THE HUSBAND.

As the apple tree among the trees of the wood, so is my beloved among the sons. I sat down under his shadow with great delight, and his fruit was sweet to my taste. (Song of Solomon 2:3 KJV)

Something is wrong if your wife does not enjoy your company or presence. In all healthy marriages, wives sincerely take pleasure in the company of their husbands. If your company annoys and irritates your wife, certainly something must be wrong. Do your search or reexamine yourself and your marital relationship.

8. A HUMBLE WIFE SINCERELY DELIGHT TO BE UNDER THE COVERING AND LEADERSHIP OF THE HUSBAND.

I sat down under his shadow with great delight, and his fruit was sweet to my taste. (Song of Solomon 2:3b KJV)

The difference between a humble wife and a proud wife is that the humble wife delights to be under the covering of her husband but the proud would not. Delight yourself as a wife under the covering of your husband. It is a sign of humility and submissiveness.

9. HAVING SEX WITH A HUSBAND MUST BE A WIFE'S DELIGHT IF THE RELATIONSHIP IS HEALTHY.

...his fruit was sweet to my taste.
(Song of Solomon 2:3c KJV)

One simple check I conduct when marriage people come before me is to ask when they last had sex—In a healthy marriage sex is a delight especially to the wife. But, in a sick marriage sex is a burden and an endurance.

10. BLESSED IS ANY HUSBAND WHOSE WIFE DELIGHTS IN HAVING SEX WITH HIM.

...his fruit was sweet to my taste.
(Song of Solomon 2:3c KJV)

A husband must count himself blessed if after many years of marriage the wife still delights in having sex with him. Do not take it for granted at all. Many wives have completely lost the delight to have sex with their husbands which must not be so at all.

11. GOING OUT WITH YOUR WIFE ONCE A WHILE TO A SPECIAL RESTAURANT, A BANQUET OR A SPECIAL OCCASION SPICE UP MARITAL RELATIONSHIP.

He brought me to the banqueting house,
and his banner over me was love.
(Song of Solomon 2:4 KJV)

Husbands must learn this act. The act of taking out your wife to eat at a special place once a while. It is really healthy and rejuvenates your marriage often.

12. ONE SICKNESS ANY HUSBAND MUST ENDEAVOR TO CURE HIS WIFE OF IS BEING "SICK OF LOVE".

Stay me with flagons, comfort me with apples: for I am sick of love.
(Song of Solomon 2:5 KJV)

A sick person is a desperate person. A sick person can loose all controls. Please never allow your wife to be sick of love. Do not withdraw your affections from your family especially your wife at any time. It is risky in any marital relationship to make ones spouse fall "Sick of Love"

13. HUSBANDS MUST LEARN TO FREQUENTLY HUG AND TOUCH THEIR WIVES (OPENLY).

His left hand is under my head, and his right hand doth embrace me.
(Song of Solomon 2:6 KJV)

One thing African husbands (Christian husbands) find difficult to do is to hug, touch, or embrace their wives openly. Let us learn this act from the couple in our study and practice them once a while. A wife feels special and loved when hugged by the husband publicly.

14. A TRUE WIFE IS ALWAYS AWARE THAT MANY WOMEN OUT THERE WISH TO BE IN HER PLACE.

I charge you, O ye daughters of Jerusalem, by the roes, and by the hinds of the field, that ye stir not up, nor awake my love, till he please. (Song of Solomon 2:7 KJV)

A wife must never take the loyalty and the commitment of her husband to her for granted. The woman in the text was aware that many women out there wished to be in her position. Protect your husband with your submissiveness to him, your love and above all your prayers.

15. NEVER FAN UP ROMANTIC PASSION IN ANOTHER PERSON'S WIFE OR HUSBAND.

I charge you, O ye daughters of Jerusalem, by the roes, and by the hinds of the field, that ye stir not up, nor awake my love, till he please. (Song of Solomon 2:7 KJV)

It is very dangerous and also an evil practice to fan up romantic passions in someone's spouse. Avoid it completely and learn to keep your distance as a married person for your own good and the good of your marriage.

16. A TRUE WIFE IS SINCERELY ANXIOUS AND RESTLESS WHEN THE HUSBAND IS NOT IN AT AN EXPECTED TIME.

The voice of my beloved! behold, he cometh leaping upon the mountains, skipping upon the hills. My beloved is like a roe or a young hart: behold, he standeth behind our wall, he looketh forth at the windows, shewing himself through the lattice. My beloved spake, and said unto me, Rise up, my love, my fair one, and come away. (Song of Solomon 2:8-10 KJV)

Husbands please do not let the persistence calls of your wife to check on your whereabout etc when you fail to get home at the time expected irritate or annoy you. All true wives become restless if their husbands are not at home at the expected time.

17. TAKING YOUR WIFE OUT ONCE A WHILE ON SIGHT SEEING IS ONE

BEAUTIFUL INGREDIENT THAT SPICE OFF MARITAL RELATIONSHIP.

My beloved spake, and said unto me, Rise up, my love, my fair one, and come away. For, lo, the winter is past, the rain is over and gone; The flowers appear on the earth; the time of the singing of birds is come, and the voice of the turtle is heard in our land; The fig tree putteth forth her green figs, and the vines with the tender grape give a good smell. Arise, my love, my fair one, and come away. O my dove, that art in the clefts of the rock, in the secret places of the stairs, let me see thy countenance, let me hear thy voice; for sweet is thy voice, and thy countenance is comely. (Song of Solomon 2:10-14 KJV)

Husbands learn to take your wives out once a while. You could simply drive to a known destination or an unknown destination. You could even go on a short holiday somewhere once a while. Just the two of you. You could also do so as a family. It is healthy.

18. ALL COUPLES MUST WORK ON THE LITTLE FOXES IN THEIR LIVES.

Take us the foxes, the little foxes, that spoil the vines: for our vines have tender grapes. (Song of Solomon 2:15 KJV)

What are little foxes? They include, little attitudes, pride, cover ups, following after vain things, carelessness, and neglecting one another. The little foxes must be checked and corrected by all couples. Such little foxes spoil the beauty of marriage.

19. A WIFE DOES NOT OWN HERSELF. SHE BELONGS TO THE HUSBAND.

My beloved is mine, and I am his: he feedeth among the lilies. (Song of Solomon 2:16 KJV)

Wives know that you do not belong to yourselves. You belong absolutely to your husband. Do not withhold yourself nor your services and duties to your husband at all. And do not play with it.

20. A HUSBAND DOES NOT OWN HIMSELF. HE BELONGS TO THE WIFE.

My beloved is mine, and I am his: he feedeth among the lilies.
(Song of Solomon 2:16 KJV)

Husbands must know that they do not belong to themselves. They belong absolutely to their wives. Husbands must never withhold themselves from their wives. They must be responsible and play their roles religiously. And must not play with it at all.

21. NO ONE CAN STAND SHARING A SPOUSE WITH ANOTHER PERSON.

My beloved is mine, and I am his: he feedeth among the lilies.
(Song of Solomon 2:16 KJV)

Couples please do not engage in any unholy relationship with another person of the opposite sex. And do avoid all appearance of such relationship. No husband and no wife can stand sharing a spouse with another person. Help yourself and help your marriage.

22. THE BEST PLACE TO ENJOY REST AND SLEEP AS MARRIED COUPLES IS IN THE ARMS OF ONE ANOTHER.

Until the day break, and the shadows flee away, turn, my beloved, and be thou like a roe or a young hart upon the mountains of Bether. (Song of Solomon 2:17 KJV)

Pleasantly receive your spouse into your arms at all times. Give your wife a shoulder to lean on. Be a pillar and a support for one another. Please always give your spouse your arms.

23. WHEN NIGHT FALLS AND HUSBAND AND WIFE ENTER THEIR BEDROOM— THEY MUST LOCK THE DOOR TO EVERY OTHER THING AND EVERY OTHER PERSON ENTIRELY.

My beloved is mine, and I am his: he feedeth among the lilies. Until the day break, and the shadows flee away, turn, my beloved, and be thou like a roe or a young hart upon the mountains of Bether. (Song of Solomon 2:16-17 KJV)

Learn to shut off the whole world when you finally retire at night into one another's arm. Put off friends. Put off phones. Put off TV and everything.

CHAPTER 3

THE WORTH OF BEING THERE

1. **IN A HEALTHY MARRIAGE THE WIFE STRUGGLE TO SLEEP WHEN THE HUSBAND IS ABSENT FOR A WHILE.**

By night on my bed I sought him whom my soul loveth: I sought him, but I found him not. (Song of Solomon 3:1 KJV)

There is a sense of restlessness on the part of one's spouse (particularly the wife) whenever the other is not around. This is normal and is to be expected. It is rather abnormal if a spouse has no such feeling.

2. NOT MISSING A SPOUSE IS ONE OF THE SIGNS THAT ALL IS NOT WELL IN THE MARITAL RELATIONSHIP.

By night on my bed I sought him whom my soul loveth: I sought him, but I found him not. (Song of Solomon 3:1 KJV)

The absence of such restlessness is a sign that all is not well in the marriage. No normal wife can live without missing the presence of the husband.

3. IN A HEALTHY MARRIAGE A WIFE WOULD DARE ALL CONSEQUENCES AND RISK FOR THE WELFARE OF THE HUSBAND.

I will rise now, and go about the city in the streets, and in the broad ways I will seek him whom my soul loveth: I sought him, but I found him not. The watchmen that go about the city found me: to whom I said, Saw ye him whom my soul loveth? It was but a little that I passed from them, but

I found him whom my soul loveth: I held him, and would not let him go, until I had brought him into my mother's house, and into the chamber of her that conceived me. (Song of Solomon 3:2-4 KJV)

This woman went around the streets in the middle of the night searching for the husband who had not been home at the time expected and might have been in a kind of problem.

4. ONE OF THE HAPPIEST MOMENT OF A WIFE IS THE VISIT OF HER HUSBAND TO HER PARENTS (MOTHER).

It was but a little that I passed from them, but I found him whom my soul loveth: I held him, and would not let him go, until I had brought him into my mother's house, and into the chamber of her that conceived me. (Song of Solomon 3:4 KJV)

Please husbands never take a visit to your wife's parents lightly. A wife is extremely happy when her husband visits her parents, especially her mother.

5. IN AN OPEN AND TRANSPARENT MARRIAGE A SPOUSE NEVER SHY AWAY FROM HIS OR HER ROOTS OR BACKGROUND.

It was but a little that I passed from them, but I found him whom my soul loveth: I held him, and would not let him go, until I had brought him into my mother's house, and into the chamber of her that conceived me. (Song of Solomon 3:4 KJV)

Your roots are your roots and you must never shy away from it. Couples must be able to take one another to their roots. You should feel good visiting your villages and the remotest parts of your birth and roots.

6. A TRUE WIFE CELEBRATES THE QUALITIES OF HER HUSBAND TO OTHERS (ESPECIALLY HER RELATIVES).

Who is this that cometh out of the wilderness like pillars of smoke, perfumed with myrrh and frankincense, with all powders of the merchant? Behold his bed, which is Solomon's; threescore valiant men are about it, of the valiant of Israel. They all hold swords, being expert in war: every man hath his sword upon his thigh because of fear in the night. King Solomon made himself a chariot of the wood of Lebanon. (Song of Solomon 3:6-9 KJV)

Couples must be able to adore one another to their families like the couple in this study. Let your relatives know how good and supportive your spouse is.

Never keep silent on that at all.

7. A TRUE WIFE IS OPENLY PROUD OF HER HUSBAND.

Who is this that cometh out of the wilderness like pillars of smoke, perfumed with myrrh and frankincense, with all powders of the merchant? Behold his bed, which is Solomon's; threescore valiant men are about it, of the valiant of Israel. They all hold swords, being expert in war: every man hath his sword upon his thigh because of fear in the night. King Solomon made himself a chariot of the wood of Lebanon. (Song of Solomon 3:6-9 KJV)

Like the Shunamite woman, all wives must be able to openly let people know of how proud they are about their husbands. This also goes for husbands.

8. A TRUE WIFE CELEBRATES THE ACHIEVEMENTS OF HER HUSBAND.

King Solomon made himself a chariot of the wood of Lebanon. He made the pillars thereof of silver, the bottom thereof of gold, the covering of it of purple, the midst thereof being paved with love, for the daughters of Jerusalem. (Song of Solomon 3:9-10 KJV)

Wives must be the first to celebrate the success, achievements, promotion, increase, and blessings of their husbands.

9. A HUSBAND MUST NOT ALLOW POSITION, ACHIEVEMENT, SUCCESS, ELEVATION TO CLOUD HIS LOVE LIFE.

He made the pillars thereof of silver, the bottom thereof of gold, the covering of it of purple, the midst thereof being paved with love, for the daughters of Jerusalem. (Song of Solomon 3:10 KJV)

Despite the position of the husband, his love life was intact. Nothing, no matter the weight or importance must take away your love life as a husband.

10. A SWEET HUSBAND MAKES THE WIFE HAPPY BY HOW HE APPEARS AND PRESENT HIMSELF IN PUBLIC.

Go forth, O ye daughters of Zion, and behold king Solomon with the crown wherewith his mother crowned him in the day of his espousals, and in the day of the gladness of his heart. (Song of Solomon 3:11 KJV)

Husbands, your appearance and conduct in public either makes your wife feel great or feel ashame. Be at your best and comport yourself well whenever in public—it is a plus in her cup.

11. A GOOD HUSBAND CELEBRATES AND APPRECIATES HIS MOTHER.

Go forth, O ye daughters of Zion, and behold king Solomon with the crown wherewith his mother crowned him in the day of his espousals, and

in the day of the gladness of his heart.
(Song of Solomon 3:11 KJV)

The husband is seen here dorning the clothes and special garments his mother gave him. He is seen celebrating and being proud of the mother. One mark of a good husband is how good he celebrates his mother. Wives, count it blessed if your husband is found of his mother. Do not fight him on that and never feel jealous about it. You have a good husband. It is only a concern when the mother dictates and seem to steer up the direction the marriage must go.

CHAPTER 4

PERTINENT AREAS OF GREAT CONCERN

1. WELL KEPT SKIN COLOUR—SONG OF SOLOMON 4:1

Behold, thou art fair, my love; behold, thou art fair; thou hast doves' eyes within thy locks: thy hair is as a flock of goats, that appear from mount Gilead. (Song of Solomon 4:1 KJV)

A wife in particular must keep her skin (skin colour) very well. No bleaching, and no excessive toning however.

2. DEVELOP DOVE EYES.

Behold, thou art fair, my love; behold, thou art fair; thou hast doves' eyes within thy locks: thy hair is as a flock of goats, that appear from mount Gilead. (Song of Solomon 4:1 KJV)

All couples must develop dove eyes. In the Bible, a dove represents purity, gentleness and peace. Couples must stop seeing evil and reading lots of evil meanings into things. See no evil, talk no evil, imagine no evil.

3. PLEASE KEEP YOUR HAIR TIDY.

Behold, thou art fair, my love; behold, thou art fair; thou hast doves' eyes within thy locks: thy hair is as a flock of goats, that appear from mount Gilead. (Song of Solomon 4:1 KJV)

This also goes for both couples but more especially wives. In the Bible, a woman's hair is a symbol of her glory [1 Cor. 11:14-15]. Please wives keep your hair clean and pleasant. Husbands too must shave properly and frequently as well as cut their hair often.

4. CHECK YOUR DENTAL CAVITY.

Thy teeth are like a flock of sheep that are even shorn, which came up from the washing; whereof every one bear twins, and none is barren among them. (Song of Solomon 4:2 KJV)

The wife in our text is praised for having a beautiful white teeth. Perfect teeth would never mar a beautiful smile. All couples must check and brush their teeth frequently and properly.

5. WATCH YOUR LIPS (MOUTH).

Thy lips are like a thread of scarlet, and thy speech is comely: thy temples are like a piece of a pomegranate within thy locks. (Song of Solomon 4:3 KJV)

The lips of a person truly adds up to his or her beauty. Husbands: Stop keeping dry and untidy lips. Check yourself in the mirror often. Wipe off your lips properly. Treat your mustache well. Wives: Carry a sweet and kissable lips. Do not make your lips dry. Check your lipsticks and apply it properly (if you do lipstick). And please do not over do your lipstick too. Stop looking like a hunger-striked Somali if you are the type that applies no lipstick.

6. BE CIRCUMSPECT WITH YOUR UTTERANCE.

Thy lips are like a thread of scarlet, and thy speech is comely: thy temples are like a piece of a pomegranate within thy locks. (Song of Solomon 4:3 KJV)

It is not just our lips that is important as couples but more importantly what comes out of our lips. The wife in this text is praised also for her comely speech. Couples must ensure that their speech is always seasoned, civil and graceful.

7. CHECK YOUR FACIAL.

Thy lips are like a thread of scarlet, and thy speech is comely: thy temples are like a piece of a pomegranate within thy locks. (Song of Solomon 4:3 KJV)

The mouth (lips) of a person is a very significant and expressive part of the face. Keep away from frowning and looking hard and unfriendly. Smile often, look tender and be a bit humorous.

8. BE VERY RESPONSIBLE (NECK).

Thy neck is like the tower of David builded for an armoury, whereon there hang a thousand bucklers, all shields of mighty men. (Song of Solomon 4:4 KJV)

The neck of a person carries the head and stands for support. So apart from keeping a beautiful neck and looking good in ones necklaces as a wife, all wives must be very responsible, up to task and very supportive to their husbands. The neck in this text also suggest strength and character. Please do not loose it.

9. Don't expose Your Breast (wife).

Thy two breasts are like two young roes that are twins, which feed among the lilies. (Song of Solomon 4:5 KJV)

A married woman must be very particular about her breast. She must not dress to reveal or expose her breast. Her breast must be special and sacred. Also, she must be very concern about examining her breast as well as avoid applying harmful substances to her breast. Finally, no man apart from your husband and your doctor has the right to touch your breast. And no man apart from your husband has the right to play with your breast.

10. ALL THE AFOREMENTIONED AREAS SPARKS ROMANCE AND MUST NOT BE TAKEN FOR GRANTED.

Behold, thou art fair, my love; behold, thou art fair; thou hast doves' eyes within thy locks: thy hair is as a flock of goats, that appear from mount Gilead. Thy teeth are like a flock of sheep that are even shorn, which came up from the washing; whereof every one bear twins, and none is barren among them. Thy lips are like a thread of scarlet, and thy speech is comely: thy temples are like a piece of a pomegranate within thy locks. Thy neck is like the tower of David builded for an armoury, whereon there hang a

thousand bucklers, all shields of mighty men.
(Song of Solomon 4:1-4 KJV)

When a couple (especially a wife) carries herself with such poise and dignity, it ends her much respect from the husband and also fuels up their romance adventures.

11. CHECK OUT AGAINST BODY SPOTS.

Thou art all fair, my love; there is no spot in thee.
(Song of Solomon 4:7 KJV)

Another area this lovely wife was praised is the fact that she had no spots. Couples must sincerely work against spots and scars in their lives. From physical spots to social spots and all forms of spots and scars. Please watch out against spots and scars on your image, your name, your person and your marriage. Spots and scars scarcely go away no matter how well you treat them.

12. TRUE LOVE IS NOT FAULT FINDING (SEES LESS FAULT).

Thouartallfair, mylove; thereisnospotinthee.
(Song of Solomon 4:7 KJV)

The husband in this scene could see no spot in his beautiful wife. This is difficult to accept. Every human being have one spot or another. The fact here is that true and sincere love sees no spots or scars. Plenty fault finding in a marital relationship is often a sign that the relation is taking a nose dive. Watch it! True love sees no fault and finds no fault.

13. NEVER BE DECEIVED BY THE HARMLESS LOOK OF A WOMAN.

Thouartallfair, mylove; thereisnospotinthee.
(Song of Solomon 4:7 KJV)

Another important fact in this text is the harmless (spotless) look of the wife.

This is virtually how most woman look. Most wives look very sweet, gentle and harmless but are actually not so to their husbands at all. As a pastor I have seen it over and over again. I pray that wives may actually be harmless not only in looks but also in their marital homes.

14. Ravish the heart of one another.

Thou hast ravished my heart, my sister, my spouse; thou hast ravished my heart with one of thine eyes, with one chain of thy neck. (Song of Solomon 4:9 KJV)

Couples must do well to commend their love towards one another. Show more love to your spouse always. Be in the hearts of one another just as in the days you were courting.

15. NEVER ALLOW YOURSELF TO BE CHARMED BY THE EYES OF ANY OTHER WOMAN APART FROM YOUR WIFE.

Thou hast ravished my heart, my sister, my spouse; thou hast ravished my heart with one of thine eyes, with one chain of thy neck. (Song of Solomon 4:9 KJV)

The charm of your spouse is all you need. Do not allow any other person to charm you. This also is a wake up call to couples (especially husbands). There are diabolic and evil women out there who actually use demonic powers to try to charm you through the medium of their eyes. Please be more prayerful and be spiritually vigilant.

16. LIVE LIKE SIBLINGS.

Thou hast ravished my heart, my sister, my spouse; thou hast ravished my heart with one of thine eyes, with one chain of thy neck.

How fair is thy love, my sister, my spouse!
how much better is thy love than wine! and
the smell of thine ointments than all spices!
(Song of Solomon 4:9-10 KJV)

The husband in this picture calls the wife 'my sister'. How beautiful marriage becomes when a husband and a wife lives like true siblings.

17. KEEP YOURSELF COMPLETELY FOR ONE ANOTHER.

A garden inclosed is my sister, my spouse;
a spring shut up, a fountain sealed.
(Song of Solomon 4:12 KJV)

Become to one another an enclosed garden. Do not allow others to come in and pluck the fruits of your romantic love. Stay faithful to your spouse and vise versa.

18. BE SEXUALLY APPEALING TO ONE ANOTHER.

Thy plants are an orchard of pomegranates, with pleasant fruits; camphire, with spikenard, Spikenard and saffron; calamus and cinnamon, with all trees of frankincense; myrrh and aloes, with all the chief spices: A fountain of gardens, a well of living waters, and streams from Lebanon. Awake, O north wind; and come, thou south; blow upon my garden, that the spices thereof may flow out. Let my beloved come into his garden, and eat his pleasant fruits. (Song of Solomon 4:13-16 KJV)

All the descriptions in this passage point to just one thing—that the spouse was so appealing. Please make yourselves appealing to each other (especially in your sex life).

19. MARITAL ROMANCE IS SUPPOSED TO REFRESH AND STRENGTHEN THE UNION.

A garden inclosed is my sister, my spouse; a spring shut up, a fountain sealed. Thy plants are an orchard of pomegranates, with pleasant fruits; camphire, with spikenard, Spikenard and saffron; calamus and cinnamon, with all trees of frankincense; myrrh and aloes, with all the chief spices: A fountain of gardens, a well of living waters, and streams from Lebanon. (Song of Solomon 4:12-15 KJV)

All the expressions in these verses are about refreshing one another in their marital and romantic union. I pray that you would find such refreshing in your love life.

20. A WIFE MUST ALWAYS BE PREPARED FOR "WAR" AND ALSO WELCOMING.

Awake, O north wind; and come, thou south; blow upon my garden, that the spices thereof may flow out. Let my beloved come into his garden, and eat his pleasant fruits. (Song of Solomon 4:16 KJV)

Although the 'garden' of ones wife is his—it is healthy that the wife invites, welcomes, and allows the husband into the garden lovingly and wholeheartedly. No true husband forces himself or breaks into his wife's 'garden' uninvited. And no true wife is begged by to husband to visit her garden. A wife must forever be ready and smilingly invite the husband into her 'garden'

CHAPTER 5

CREATE A HEALTHY HOME

1. IN A HEALTHY MARRIAGE ONE IS OF A HIGH SPIRIT AND EXTREMELY EXCITED IN HIS OR HER MATRIMONIAL HOME.

I am come into my garden, my sister, my spouse: I have gathered my myrrh with my spice; I have eaten my honeycomb with my honey; I have drunk my wine with my milk: eat, O friends; drink, yea, drink abundantly, O beloved. (Song of Solomon 5:1 KJV)

The woman in our context is seen in this verse as a wife full of life, enthusiasm and high spirit in her own matrimonial home. Something is certainly not right when a spouse (particularly a wife) is low spirited in her matrimonial home.

2. GOOD AND ABUNDANT SUPPLY OF LOGISTICS AT HOME SPICE UP MARRIAGE.

I am come into my garden, my sister, my spouse: I have gathered my myrrh with my spice; I have eaten my honeycomb with my honey; I have drunk my wine with my milk: eat, O friends; drink, yea, drink abundantly, O beloved. (Song of Solomon 5:1 KJV)

Not only was the wife of high spirit at home. She explains that there was abundance of food and goodies in the house. It is essential that couples (especially husbands) ensure that there is plenty foodstuff and enough logistics in the house. This is one essential ingredient that sparks up the light in the home.

3. IN A GOOD AND A HEALTHY HOME THERE IS ALWAYS PREPARED FOOD.

I am come into my garden, my sister, my spouse: I have gathered my myrrh with my spice; I have eaten my honeycomb with my honey; I have drunk my wine with my milk: eat, O friends; drink, yea, drink abundantly, O beloved. (Song of Solomon 5:1 KJV)

We deduce from this verse that there were also prepared meals in the house. Not only must there be plenty provision of food in the house, a wife must ensure that there is always 'eatable' (prepared) food. These all help spark up the fire of live and love in the house.

4. IN A LIVING AND HEALTHY MARRIAGE ONE FREELY ENJOYS THE FACILITIES AND THE GOODIES IN THE HOME

WITHOUT ANY SENSE OF ANXIETY OR A SENSE OF RESTRICTION.

I am come into my garden, my sister, my spouse: I have gathered my myrrh with my spice; I have eaten my honeycomb with my honey; I have drunk my wine with my milk: eat, O friends; drink, yea, drink abundantly, O beloved. (Song of Solomon 5:1 KJV)

The Shunamite woman is depicted eating freely and drinking the milk in the house. How sweet that is. She needs not write a letter asking for permission to eat something in her house. May this be the nature and scene in the homes of christian couples.

5. **IN A HEALTHY AND GOOD SPIRITED MARRIAGE OR HOME, FRIENDS AND**

LOVED ONES COULD BE INVITED FOR DINNER.

I am come into my garden, my sister, my spouse: I have gathered my myrrh with my spice; I have eaten my honeycomb with my honey; I have drunk my wine with my milk: eat, O friends; drink, yea, drink abundantly, O beloved. (Song of Solomon 5:1 KJV)

The Shunamite woman is seen inviting her friends to come to her house and eat freely. This is another sign of a lovely and healthy home. A place where one is at liberty once a while to welcome friends and loved ones to share a meal with them.

6. A HUSBAND MUST BE WELCOME HOME AS A KING.

I sleep, but my heart waketh: it is the voice of my beloved that knocketh, saying, Open to me, my sister, my love, my dove, my

*undefiled: for my head is filled with dew,
and my locks with the drops of the night.
(Song of Solomon 5:2 KJV)*

When a husband comes home from work or from a journey, a true wife must quickly jump up and move to warmly and affectionately welcome him. No wife must ever play with this and so must husbands.

7. PETTY EXCUSES FROM A SPOUSE SPOILS A LOT OF THINGS IN MARRIAGE.

I have put off my coat; how shall I put it on? I have washed my feet; how shall I defile them? (Song of Solomon 5:3 KJV)

The wife in this scene was making excuses and the husband went away by the time she got up to open the door for him. Do not make excuses and never be too lazy on your spouse.

8. Petty delays in doing things at the right time might be too late.

I opened to my beloved; but my beloved had withdrawn himself, and was gone: my soul failed when he spake: I sought him, but I could not find him; I called him, but he gave me no answer. (Song of Solomon 5:6 KJV)

Not only did the wife give petty excuses, she was also too slow in responding to the husband. Such petty delays from a spouse could cause one's marital relation dearly. Couples must be prompt in responding to one another. Never be slow or turn a deaf ear to the voice and demands of your spouse.

9. PETTY EXCUSES AND DELAYS MIGHT END UP IN UNBEARABLE HURTS AND PAINS.

The watchmen that went about the city found me, they smote me, they wounded me; the keepers of the walls took away my veil from me. I charge you, O daughters of Jerusalem, if ye find my beloved, that ye tell him, that I am sick of love. (Song of Solomon 5:7-8 KJV)

Precious time is wasted when we delay or make excuses. Sometimes great and unrepairable damages are done to our marital relationships as we keep delaying and making excuses. In this scene when the wife went out after the delays to look for the husband, she was arrested and treated bad. She paid dearly for her delays and excuses.

10. YOU SHOULD HAVE A VERY CLEAR PICTURE (SOMETIMES ITEMIZED) OF

WHAT MAKES YOUR SPOUSE STAND OUT.

What is thy beloved more than another beloved, O thou fairest among women? what is thy beloved more than another beloved, that thou dost so charge us? My beloved is white and ruddy, the chiefest among ten thousand. His head is as the most fine gold, his locks are bushy, and black as a raven. His eyes are as the eyes of doves by the rivers of waters, washed with milk, and fitly set. His cheeks are as a bed of spices, as sweet flowers: his lips like lilies, dropping sweet smelling myrrh. His hands are as gold rings set with the beryl: his belly is as bright ivory overlaid with sapphires. His legs are as pillars of marble, set upon sockets of fine gold: his countenance is as Lebanon, excellent as the cedars. His mouth is most sweet: yea, he is altogether lovely. This is my beloved, and this is my friend, O daughters of Jerusalem. (Song of Solomon 5:9-16 KJV)

The woman in the text tells the other women why her beloved was so special and irreplaceable. There are reasons why you married your spouse. And there are very many good things you have found out about him whilst married. Like the couple in this study, every spouse must be able to silently put down all the good qualities in the other person. These are the real blocks and stones (strong reasons) of your marriage. Do it now!

11. ALWAYS FOCUS ON THE POSITIVE ATTRIBUTES OF YOUR SPOUSE.

What is thy beloved more than another beloved, O thou fairest among women? what is thy beloved more than another beloved, that thou dost so charge us? My beloved is white and ruddy, the chiefest among ten thousand. His head is as the most fine gold, his locks are bushy, and black as a raven. His eyes are as the eyes of doves by the rivers of waters, washed with milk, and fitly set. His cheeks are as a bed of spices, as sweet flowers: his lips like lilies, dropping sweet smelling myrrh. His hands are as gold rings set with the beryl: his belly is as bright ivory overlaid with sapphires. His legs are as pillars of marble, set upon sockets of fine gold: his countenance is as Lebanon, excellent as the cedars. His mouth is most sweet: yea, he is altogether lovely. This is my beloved, and this is my friend, O daughters of Jerusalem. (Song of Solomon 5:9-16 KJV)

In giving out the attributes of her beloved to the other women, she focused entirely on the positive attributes of the husband. All couples must learn this. If you learn to focus on the positive attributes of your spouse you would be more happier than concentrating on the negatives.

12. NEVER TRADE OUT THE NEGATIVE ATTRIBUTES OF YOUR SPOUSE

**TO FRIENDS AND OUTSIDERS
UNNECESSARILY.**

What is thy beloved more than another beloved, O thou fairest among women? what is thy beloved more than another beloved, that thou dost so charge us? My beloved is white and ruddy, the chiefest among ten thousand. His head is as the most fine gold, his locks are bushy, and black as a raven. His eyes are as the eyes of doves by the rivers of waters, washed with milk, and fitly set. His cheeks are as a bed of spices, as sweet flowers: his lips like lilies, dropping sweet smelling myrrh. His hands are as gold rings set with the beryl: his belly is as bright ivory overlaid with sapphires. His legs are as pillars of marble, set upon sockets of fine gold: his countenance is as Lebanon, excellent as the cedars. His mouth is most sweet: yea, he is altogether lovely. This is my beloved, and this is my friend, O daughters of Jerusalem. (Song of Solomon 5:9-16 KJV)

In describing the husband to other women, the Shunamite woman never mentioned one negative attribute of him. Does it mean he had no flaws? Certainly no! The lesson is that no spouse is permitted to trade the negative attributes of the other to mere friends and outsiders.

CHAPTER 6

APPRECIATE ONE ANOTHER HIGHLY

1. Security in marriage is very needful.

I am my beloved's, and my beloved is mine: he feedeth among the lilies. (Song of Solomon 6:3 KJV)

The wife knew for sure that she belonged to her beloved husband. Thus, all her affections are surely for her husband alone. And all the affections of the husband are for her alone.

2. A WIFE MUST NEVER FOCUS ON JUST ONE SIDE OF HER BEAUTY.

Thou art beautiful, O my love, as Tirzah, comely as Jerusalem, terrible as an army with banners. (Song of Solomon 6:4 KJV)

Tirzah was a city known for it's great beauty. Tirzah then stood for pleasantness. Thus, a wife must be pleasing, wholesome in appearance, and attractive.

3. A WIFE MUST EXHIBIT BEAUTY IN THREEFOLD.

Thou art beautiful, O my love, as Tirzah, comely as Jerusalem, terrible as an army with banners. (Song of Solomon 6:4 KJV)

A wife must be known for her great beauty in the following three areas:
i. Natural Beauty

ii. Pleasant, Sweet, Lovely and graceful

iii. Strong, firm, wonderful and awesome

4. A WIFE MUST BE IMPOSING.

Turn away thine eyes from me, for they have overcome me: thy hair is as a flock of goats that appear from Gilead. (Song of Solomon 6:5 KJV)

The wife in this study was described as terrible as an army with banners. This expression meant she was awesome, breathtaking, and imposing. Simply put, she conquered his heart 'koraa' (absolutely).

5. COUPLES MUST BE ABLE TO POINT OUT SOMETHING IN THEIR SPOUSE THAT CAPTIVATES THEM.

Turn away thine eyes from me, for they have overcome me: thy hair is as a flock of goats that appear from Gilead. Thy teeth are as a flock of sheep which go up from the washing, whereof every one beareth twins, and there is not one barren among them. As a piece of a pomegranate are thy temples within thy locks. (Song of Solomon 6:5-7 KJV)

Somethings like great and good character of one's spouse, tenderness towards one another, passionate love for one another, the confidence of a spouse, and peculiar grace upon one's spouse could be captivating to one another. Do your own check list now.

6. PREFERRING ONE'S WIFE ABOVE ALL OTHERS IS WHAT EVERY WIFE DESIRES IN A HUSBAND.

There are threescore queens, and fourscore concubines, and virgins without number. (Song of Solomon 6:8 KJV)

A true and dependable husband must be able to decide firmly that; there are many beautiful queens and 'concubines' (girls who wish he falls for them) in the world, but he still stand for his wife—and that none of them can be compared to his wife.

7. A WIFE MUST KNOW AND KEEP IN MIND THAT SHE WAS CHOSEN (INTO MARRIAGE) BY GRACE.

There are threescore queens, and fourscore concubines, and virgins without number. (Song of Solomon 6:8 KJV)

The reality is that before your husband settled on you there were more powerful women out there who wished they were the ones settled on. And even whilst you are in the marriage, there are still many striking women out there who wish to take your place. You were chosen by grace—do not play about it. Many highly classed and well to do women are desperately looking for it in vain.

8. A WIFE MUST CONSTANTLY HOLD HER HUSBAND DEAR AND TREAT HIM WELL KNOWING THERE ARE A THOUSAND AND ONE WOMEN OUT THERE WHO ARE EYING THE SAME MAN.

There are threescore queens, and fourscore concubines, and virgins without number. (Song of Solomon 6:8 KJV)

Mrs. Wife, please treat your husband like a king. There are women who are prepared to remove his socks from his feet, kiss his smelling toes, take him into the shower, pamper him like a baby, and welcome him into their garden. Do not allow your meanness to push him out into the hands of these hunters.

9. THE STRUGGLE TO LIVE CHASTE COULD BE VERY UNBEARABLE ON A WELL ENDOWED HUSBAND.

There are threescore queens, and fourscore concubines, and virgins without number. (Song of Solomon 6:8 KJV)

The competition on a less endowed husband might not be that much. But great is the competition on a man that is well endowed—endowed financially, endowed with good looks, endowed with position, endowed with a gift or talent, endowed with some property or inheritance, endowed with green card , endowed with fame etc. Pray for your husband, and much more protect him with your character of love, care, understanding, and submissiveness.

10. AN UNDEFILED WIFE IS A GREAT ASSET TO ANY HUSBAND.

My dove, my undefiled is but one; she is the only one of her mother, she is the choice one of her that bare her. The daughters saw her, and blessed her; yea, the queens and the concubines, and they praised her. (Song of Solomon 6:9 KJV)

Not only must a husband be chaste, a wife must be undefiled. Undefiled in this context means, without blemish, upright, perfect, spotless, whole, sincere, complete, unsoiled. Such a wife is a priceless gift. Try to live it.

11. COUPLES PLEASE TREAT ONE ANOTHER AS SOMEONE'S SPECIAL CHILD.

My dove, my undefiled is but one; she is the only one of her mother, she is the choice one of her that bare her. The daughters saw her, and blessed her; yea, the queens

and the concubines, and they praised her.
(Song of Solomon 6:9 KJV)

The husband mentions in this text that his wife is the only daughter of her mother, and therefore very special to the mother. Couples, please be careful how you treat one another. Your spouse is so dear to his or her family. Do not treat him or her anyhow. He or she might be the light of his or her family. If they hear you treat him or her mean they would descend on you both physically, spiritually, and diabolically.

12. A TRUE HUSBAND FEELS VERY PROUD WHEN HIS WIFE IS CELEBRATED AND PRAISED.

My dove, my undefiled is but one; she is the only one of her mother, she is the choice one of her that bare her. The daughters saw her, and blessed her; yea, the queens and the concubines, and they praised her. Who is she that looketh forth as the morning, fair as the moon, clear as the sun, and terrible as an army with banners? I went down into the garden of nuts to see the fruits of the valley, and to see whether the vine flourished, and the pomegranates budded. Or ever I was aware, my soul made me like the chariots of Amminadib. (Song of Solomon 6:9-12 KJV)

The husband declares how much his wife was admired by all that had acquaintance with her like her mother, the other women and friends, the queens, and even the concubines. They all blessed her, praise her, and celebrated her.

CHAPTER 7

OPEN THE GATES OF BATHRABBIM

1. A WIFE MUST HAVE A BEAUTIFUL FEET.

How beautiful are thy feet with shoes, O prince's daughter! the joints of thy thighs are like jewels, the work of the hands of a cunning workman. (Song of Solomon 7:1 KJV)

In this text, the husband continue to extol the virtues of his wife. He speaks of her beautiful feet. The beautiful feet here could stand for a number of things. Three striking ones are:

- Her feet in shoes fit so perfectly. Ladies have a craving for shoes.

Husbands understand, and praise them when they were them.

- Her gracious steps as a lady. Wives must be allowed to graciously take their steps. They must not be forced to march like 'congo soldiers'.

- Her going forth. Wives must carefully watch their going forth. It might not be expedient for a wife to go anywhere.

2. A couple (especially a husband) must know the exact anatomic form of his wife. This is also very romantic on his part.

Thy navel is like a round goblet, which wanteth not liquor: thy belly is like an heap of wheat set about with lilies. Thy two breasts are like two young roes that are twins. Thy neck is as a tower of ivory; thine eyes like the fishpools in Heshbon, by the gate of Bathrabbim: thy nose is as the

*tower of Lebanon which looketh toward Damascus. Thine head upon thee is like Carmel, and the hair of thine head like purple; the king is held in the galleries. How fair and how pleasant art thou, O love, for delights! This thy stature is like to a palm tree, and thy breasts to clusters of grapes.
(Song of Solomon 7:2-7 KJV)*

This husband was conversant with every part of the wife. She had a princely disposition. She was all glorious within and without. How much do you known about your wife body? What is her shoe size, her dress size etc. Many husbands are at fault here.

3. WIVES TREASURE YOUR BREAST DEARLY FOR YOUR HUSBAND'S SAKE.

*Thy two breasts are like two young roes that are twins.
(Song of Solomon 7:3 KJV)*

The wife's breast is refereed to eight times in Song of Solomon [1:13, 4:5, 7:3 7:8, 8:1, 8:8, 8:10]. All women (especially wives) must know how sacred and special their breasts are and thereby respect these two special features on their body.

4. A WIFE MUST HAVE CLEAR EYES.

Thy neck is as a tower of ivory; thine eyes like the fishpools in Heshbon, by the gate of Bathrabbim: thy nose is as the tower of Lebanon which looketh toward Damascus. (Song of Solomon 7:4 KJV)

Eyes like the fish-pool in Heshbon is different from having dove eyes. In this instant, it indicates having depth of intelligence. A wife must be very intelligent.

5. A WIFE MUST BE A DAUGHTER OF MANY.

Thy neck is as a tower of ivory; thine eyes like the fishpools in Heshbon, by the gate of Bathrabbim: thy nose is as the tower of Lebanon which looketh toward Damascus. (Song of Solomon 7:4 KJV)

Here we come across the gate of Bathrabbim. This gate is referred to as the gate of the city full of people (Lam 1:1). By describing his wife with this word [Bathrabbim], the husband was simply referring to the wife as a daughter of many. In other words, a woman who loves people and has many daughters around her. A wife, must love people and never be irritated receiving guests or people into her house. Her gates must be opened to many people, especially guests of her husband.

6. A WIFE MUST HAVE THE CHARM OF STATELINESS.

How fair and how pleasant art thou, O love, for delights!
(Song of Solomon 7:6 KJV)

This wife was very graceful, feminine, and have the charm of stateliness. The husband must never feel embarrassed taking her out (especially to official and stately occasions). She must be well comported, sociable, intelligent, enjoy conversing, able to contribute meaningfully on issues, and simply a delight to the husband on such high profile platforms. Husbands help your wives to that pedigree if they are not there yet.

7. BAD BREATH IS NOT SEXY.

I said, I will go up to the palm tree, I will take hold of the boughs thereof: now

also thy breasts shall be as clusters of the
vine, and the smell of thy nose like apples;
(Song of Solomon 7:8 KJV)

It is mentioned here again that the husband was attracted by the sweet fragrance of the wife. In this text, the focus is more on the fragrance of the husband's breath. Bad Breath can be devastating. Lets help one another out of this as spouses.

8. IT IS A GREAT BLESSING FOR YOUR HUSBAND TO DESIRE YOU.

I am my beloved's, and his desire is toward me.
(Song of Solomon 7:10 KJV)

The wife points out here that all the desire of the husband is towards her. Blessed are you if your husband so desires you. Many husbands desire other figures in skirt than their own wives. Pray your husband desires you alone.

9. A WIFE MUST NEVER KILL THE DESIRE OF HER HUSBAND TOWARD HER.

Come, my beloved, let us go forth into the field; let us lodge in the villages. Let us get up early to the vineyards; let us see if the vine flourish, whether the tender grape appear, and the pomegranates bud forth: there will I give thee my loves. The mandrakes give a smell, and at our gates are all manner of pleasant fruits, new and old, which I have laid up for thee, O my beloved. (Song of Solomon 7:11-13 KJV)

As a wife, once you perceive that your husband heartily loves you and yearn strongly for an intimacy you must not push him away nor act in a way that would kill that desire. When a man's desire towards the wife gradually dies of—the marriage is alive but dead. Dear sister never contribute to killing the desire of your husband towards you, it may be hard to resurrect it.

10. A WIFE MUST WHOLE HEARTEDLY WELCOME THE DESIRE OF HER HUSBAND TOWARDS HER.

Come, my beloved, let us go forth into the field; let us lodge in the villages. (Song of Solomon 7:11 KJV)

A wife must anticipate the visit of the husband into her 'garden' always. A wife must receive the husband with all earnestness into her 'garden' always. She must be willing to prepare for him all kinds of fruits. Her constant slogans must always be; 'come my beloved!', 'are you okay?' 'do you want more?''

CHAPTER 8

A WALL OR A DOOR?

1. A TRUE HUSBAND IS LIKE A BIG AND A CARING BROTHER TO THE WIFE.

O that thou wert as my brother, that sucked the breasts of my mother! when I should find thee without, I would kiss thee; yea, I should not be despised. (Song of Solomon 8:1 KJV)

Living together with such a brother and being under the care and covering of such a brother is more to be desired. A wife would always like to live in the same house and spend precious time together with such a husband.

2. ONE OF THE GREATEST JOY OF A WIFE IS THE VISIT TO HER PARENTS BY THE HUSBAND.

I would lead thee, and bring thee into my mother's house, who would instruct me: I would cause thee to drink of spiced wine of the juice of my pomegranate. (Song of Solomon 8:2 KJV)

A wife is extremely honored and feel highly respected and loved whenever the husband visits together with her to her mother. It is a great display of affection to a wife that a husband must not underestimate at all.

3. COUPLES MUST NEVER FORGET HOW THEY BEGAN AND WHERE IT ALL STARTED.

Who is this that cometh up from the wilderness, leaning upon her beloved? I raised thee up under the apple tree: there thy mother brought thee forth: there

*she brought thee forth that bare thee.
(Song of Solomon 8:5 KJV)*

In this text the husband is recalling the first time they met. He also mentions that they first met under an apple tree. Couples must have fonding memories of where and how they first met. Possibly, take an excursion occasionally to such a place.

4. A WIFE IS INDEED HAPPY AND SECURED IF SHE KNOWS SHE IS NOT COMPETING WITH ANYONE FOR YOUR HEART.

*Set me as a seal upon thine heart, as a seal upon thine arm: for love is strong as death; jealousy is cruel as the grave: the coals thereof are coals of fire, which hath a most vehement flame.
(Song of Solomon 8:6 KJV)*

The best security any wife looks for in a marriage is NO COMPETITION. Give your wife this best security and assurance. Keep away from other ladies. Avoid all hidden relationships. Let your wife know she is the only one.

5. SIGNETS, EMBLEMS, AND TOKENS OF LOVE MATTERS GREATLY.

Set me as a seal upon thine heart, as a seal upon thine arm: for love is strong as death; jealousy is cruel as the grave: the coals thereof are coals of fire, which hath a most vehement flame. (Song of Solomon 8:6 KJV)

A wife is in high spirit when she sees signets of love and her emblems (photos) around the husband—for example if the husband always wear his wedding ring, keep her picture on his office desk, or use her photo for his profile picture (dp), etc. The Shunamite woman like all wives wanted this assurance that she occupied the first place of her husband.

6. HUSBANDS PLEASE NEVER PLAY WITH THE LOVE OF YOUR WIFE...IT IS SUICIDAL!

Set me as a seal upon thine heart, as a seal upon thine arm: for love is strong as death; jealousy is cruel as the grave: the coals thereof are coals of fire, which hath a most vehement flame. Many waters cannot quench love, neither can the floods drown it: if a man would give all the substance of his house for love, it would utterly be contemned. (Song of Solomon 8:6-7 KJV)

The strength and fervency of a wife's love is unparalleled. It is unquenchable. It is undrownable. It is unconquerable. It is unbreakable. And it is untamable. To joke with her love is like trying to bury her alive.

7. Love's jealousy: A wife's jealousy can be very unyielding and very cruel.

Set me as a seal upon thine heart, as a seal upon thine arm: for love is strong as death; jealousy is cruel as the grave: the coals thereof are coals of fire, which hath a most vehement flame. (Song of Solomon 8:6 KJV)

Husbands do not give room for your wife to be jealous. A jealous wife is terrible. She can do anything. Please you have no idea how far your wife can go if she gets jealous. So do not create room for her to put on her jealousy garment at all.

8. True love is not for sale.

Many waters cannot quench love, neither can the floods drown it: if a man would give all the substance of his house for love, it would utterly be contemned. (Song of Solomon 8:7 KJV)

To attempt to buy your spouse's (particularly your wife's) love is to violate her personality. No marriage works properly on such foundation. The woman in this study stated that she would utterly pour contempt on such a move.

9. COUPLES MUST PUT PRICELESS VALUE ON THEIR MARRIAGE UNION.

Many waters cannot quench love, neither can the floods drown it: if a man would give all the substance of his house for love, it would utterly be contemned. (Song of Solomon 8:7 KJV)

Husbands and wives need to value the love in their hearts dearly. Nothing must be able to buy their love. Their love must be priceless love.

10. A CHASTE AND A PURE WIFE IS SIMPLY PRICELESS.

If she be a wall, we will build upon her a palace of silver: and if she be a door, we will inclose her with boards of cedar. (Song of Solomon 8:9 KJV)

The brothers of the Shunamite woman assured her whilst she was a very young girl that she grows up to become a wall, at the time she is being given out in marriage they shall proudly honour her. How blessed a husband is if the wife she marries is a 'wall'—chaste and pure. Such women are gradually becoming scarce in this time and age. The shulamite asserts that she had kept herself pure (vs 10).

11. WOE IS ANY HUSBAND WHOSE WIFE IS PROMISCUOUS.

If she be a wall, we will build upon her a palace of silver: and if she be a door, we will inclose her with boards of cedar. (Song of Solomon 8:9 KJV)

The brothers of the Shunamite woman however warned her whilst she was a very young girl that if she grows up to become a promiscuous lady and easily accessibly by all men like a door, then they would be forced to put restrictions on her path. How I pity any husband who marries such a door-like woman as wife.

12. A REAL DEPENDABLE WIFE IS A 'WALL-LIKE' WIFE.

I am a wall, and my breasts like towers: then was I in his eyes as one that found favour. (Song of Solomon 8:10 KJV)

A chaste and disciplined wife is as impregnable as a strong castle wall. Such is a truly dependable wife.

AUTHOR

BONIFACE KEELSON is a preacher of the Gospel of Christ. He was raised in the Lord in Scripture Union, and has served in various capacities of leadership in the union from secondary school days through the University. He also served as the Assemblies of God Campus ministry President at the University of Ghana-Legon in the year 1996-1997.

Boniface holds a diploma in Theology from the Southern Ghana Bible College, Saltpond. He also holds a Masters in Missions degree from the University of Wales. He was commissioned an Evangelist with full ministerial rights in 2005. He is the leader and minister-in-charge of the Fresh Grace (Assemblies of God) Prayer Ground at Brekumanso near Asamankese.

He is a Revivalist and travels far and near with the word of God.

Currently, he is based in Canada as a missionary of Assemblies of God, Ghana, serving as the pastor-in-charge of Lighthouse Assembly of God, Toronto. His home church in Ghana is the Triumph Centre Assembly of God, Dzorwulu, Accra. Boniface is married to Evelyn Ama Obenewaa and the two of them are seriously involved in the work of God.